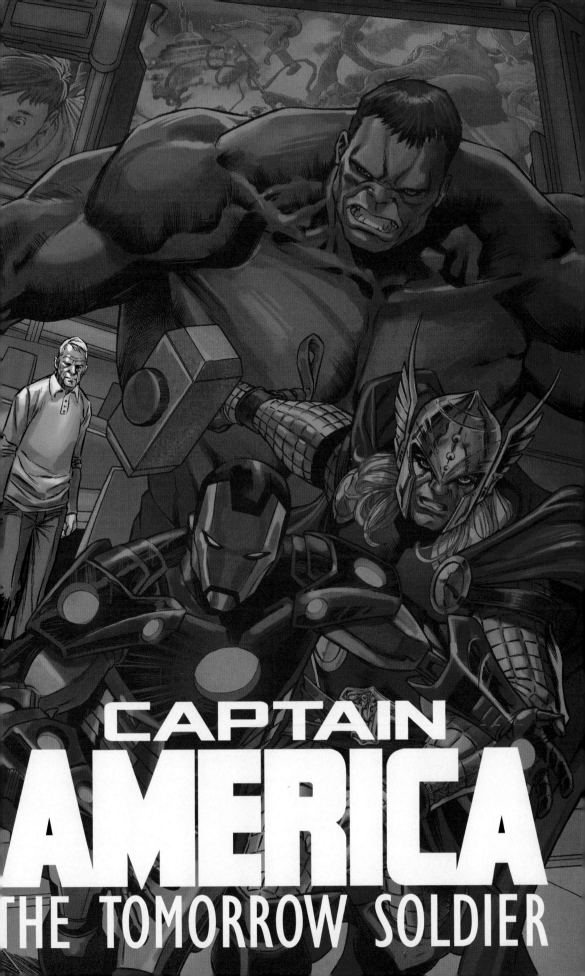

CAPTAIN AMERICA
THE TOMORROW SOLDIER

THE TOMORROW SOLDIER

COLLECTION EDITOR
JENNIFER GRÜNWALD

ASSISTANT EDITOR
SARAH BRUNSTAD

ASSOCIATE MANAGING EDITOR
ALEX STARBUCK

EDITOR, SPECIAL PROJECTS
MARK D. BEAZLEY

SENIOR EDITOR,
SPECIAL PROJECTS
JEFF YOUNGQUIST

SVP PRINT, SALES
& MARKETING
DAVID GABRIEL

BOOK DESIGNER
NELSON RIBEIRO

EDITOR IN CHIEF
AXEL ALONSO

CHIEF CREATIVE OFFICER
JOE QUESADA

PUBLISHER
DAN BUCKLEY

EXECUTIVE PRODUCER
ALAN FINE

WRITER
RICK REMENDER

PENCILERS
CARLOS PACHECO
WITH PAUL RENAUD (#24)
& STUART IMMONEN (#25)

INKERS
MARIANO TAIBO
WITH PAUL RENAUD (#24)
& WADE VON GRAWBADGER (#25)

COLORISTS
DEAN WHITE
WITH LEE LOUGHRIDGE (#22),
SONIA OBACK (#24),
VERONICA GANDINI (#25)
& MARTE GRACIA (#25)

LETTERER
VC'S JOE CARAMAGNA

COVER ART
CARLOS PACHECO & DEAN WHITE (#22-24)
AND STUART IMMONEN,
WADE VON GRAWBADGER
& MARTE GRACIA (#25)

ASSISTANT EDITOR
JAKE THOMAS

EDITOR
TOM BREVOORT

CAPTAIN AMERICA CREATED BY JOE SIMON & JACK KIRBY

CAPTAIN AMERICA VOL. 5: THE TOMORROW SOLDIER. Contains material originally published in magazine form as CAPTAIN AMERICA #22-25 and MARVEL 75TH ANNIVERSARY CELEBRATION #1. First printing 2014. ISBN# 978-0-7851-8955-8. Published by MARVEL WORLDWIDE, INC., a subsidiary of MARVEL ENTERTAINMENT, LLC. OFFICE OF PUBLICATION: 135 West 50th Street, New York, NY 10020. Copyright © 2014 Marvel Characters, Inc. All rights reserved. All characters featured in this issue and the distinctive names and likenesses thereof, and all related indicia are trademarks of Marvel Characters, Inc. No similarity between any of the names, characters, persons, and/or institutions in this magazine with those of any living or dead person or institution is intended, and any such similarity which may exist is purely coincidental. **Printed in the U.S.A.** ALAN FINE, EVP - Office of the President, Marvel Worldwide, Inc. and EVP & CMO Marvel Characters B.V.; DAN BUCKLEY, Publisher & President - Print, Animation & Digital Divisions; JOE QUESADA, Chief Creative Officer; TOM BREVOORT, SVP of Publishing; DAVID BOGART, SVP of Operations & Procurement, Publishing; C.B. CEBULSKI, SVP of Creator & Content Development; DAVID GABRIEL, SVP Print, Sales & Marketing; JIM O'KEEFE, VP of Operations & Logistics; DAN CARR, Executive Director of Publishing Technology; SUSAN CRESPI, Editorial Operations Manager; ALEX MORALES, Publishing Operations Manager; STAN LEE, Chairman Emeritus. For information regarding advertising in Marvel Comics or on Marvel.com, please contact Niza Disla, Director of Marvel Partnerships, at ndisla@marvel.com. For Marvel subscription inquiries, please call 800-217-9158. **Manufactured between 10/24/2014 and 12/8/2014 by R.R. DONNELLEY, INC., SALEM, VA, USA.**

10 9 8 7 6 5 4 3 2 1

During WWII a secret military experiment turned scrawny Steve Rogers into America's first super-soldier, Captain America. Near the end of the war Rogers was presumed dead in an explosion over the English Channel.

Decades later Captain America was found frozen in ice and revived. Steve Rogers awakened to a world he never imagined, a man out of time. He again took up the mantle of Captain America, defending the U.S. and the world from threats of all kinds.

PREVIOUSLY...

aptain America was kidnapped by Arnim Zola and brought to Dimension Z, where Zola uled as a harsh dictator. Zola wanted to use the Super-Soldier Serum in Cap's genetic ode to make his own race of super-beings, but Cap broke free before he could finish his xperiments, taking Zola's infant child Ian with him. After spending ten years in Dimension raising Ian as his own, Cap defeated Zola and escaped with Jet Black, Zola's daughter, but st both lost both his lover Sharon Carter and Ian.

pon his return Cap, with the help of Sam WIlson, a.k.a. the Falcon, worked to train Jet Black be a hero. In a battle with the Iron Nail, a former S.H.I.E.L.D. agent who attempted to verthrow the powerhouses of the West, the Super-Soldier Serum within Captain America was eutralized, causing him to age rapidly into an old man!

TWENTY-TWO

A LONE FIGURE EMERGES, SURVEYING THIS ALIEN LANDSCAPE.

A COMPUTER WHIRRS FOR A MOMENT BEFORE INDICATING THE LOCATION OF HIS TARGET.

HE HAS BEEN WAITING YEARS FOR THIS MOMENT.

TRAINED ALL HIS LIFE FOR IT.

HIS MISSION HOLDS GRAVE IMPORTANCE.

HIS LOYALTY UNWAVERING.

HE WILL NOT FAIL.

CAPTAIN AMERICA IS ANOTHER PATSY, ANOTHER TOOL OF THE MILITARY-INDUSTRIAL COMPLEX THAT HAS TAKEN OVER OUR NATION.

MRS. SPENDAL, IT'S WELL-DOCUMENTED THAT S.H.I.E.L.D. AND CAPTAIN AMERICA HAVE **SAVED OUR WORLD** FROM SOME MANNER OF INSANITY OR ANOTHER A **DOZEN** TIMES.

ARE YOU SUGGESTING WE **RETIRE** CAPTAIN AMERICA AND **SHUT DOWN** S.H.I.E.L.D.?

I THINK **ANYBODY** WHO'S REPRESENTING OUR NATION TO THE ENTIRE WORLD SHOULD BE HELD ACCOUNTABLE TO THE VOTERS.

THEY SHOULD BE **ELECTED**.

STEVE ROGERS IS A RELIC AND HE **DOESN'T** REPRESENT MY POINT OF VIEW!

HE **DOESN'T** UNDERSTAND THE COMPLEXITIES OF THE MODERN WORLD!

AND AFTER NROSVEKISTAN, HOW **ANYONE** COULD TRUST HIM AGAIN IS **BEYOND** ME, GALE. AND MOST PEOPLE I KNOW **AGREE** WITH ME--

CLIKK

YOU CAN'T WATCH THIS STUFF, CAP...

...IT'S ACID.

IT'LL CORRODE YOUR BRAIN.

IT'S JUST SOME TERRIFIED PEOPLE, ANGRY BECAUSE THEY DON'T UNDERSTAND THE ENTIRE STORY.

JUMPING TO THE WORST POSSIBLE CONCLUSIONS ABOUT YOU.

EVERYBODY LOVES TO ASSUME THOSE IN CHARGE ARE CORRUPT.

I'M BEGINNING TO SEE THEIR POINT, MARIA.

DID YOU RECOVER MY SHIELD?

WE HAVE, BUT IT'S HIGHLY RADIOACTIVE RIGHT NOW.

WE'RE WORKING ON A WAY TO DECONTAMINATE IT.

THE GOOD NEWS JUST KEEPS ON COMING.

YOU STOPPED WORLD WAR III, THERE'S NO QUESTION ABOUT THAT, CAP.

YOU STOPPED THE IRON NAIL, SAVED COUNTLESS LIVES.

YOU SAVED YOUR NATION'S REPUTATION AND PREVENTED WHAT WOULD HAVE SURELY LED TO THE COLLAPSE OF OUR UNION.

PRETTY GOOD DAY OF WORK.

YOU MAY WELL HAVE SACRIFICED YOUR YOUTH TO STOP THAT MADMAN.

YOU DON'T DESERVE TO BE ATTACKED.

YOU DON'T DESERVE ANY OF THIS, STEVE.

CAN'T SMOKE IN HERE, FURY.

IT'S BEEF JERKY. ORGANIC. GRASS FED.

FINE.

SO, WHAT HAPPENS NOW? WHAT HAPPENS TO GUNGNIR?

IT'S BACK AT THE SAHARA STATION.

BEING REPAIRED.

YOU'RE NOT DESTROYING IT?!

NO. WE'RE NOT.

MAYBE RAN SHEN WAS **RIGHT** ABOUT S.H.I.E.L.D.!

MAYBE YOU **HAVE** GROWN TOO POWERFUL FOR YOUR OWN GOOD.

THIS IS **INSANE!**

HOW INSANE IS IT?

HOW INSANE IS IT TO BUILD SOMETHING THAT WE CAN USE TO **PROTECT OURSELVES** THE NEXT TIME A **CELESTIAL EXECUTIONER** SHOWS UP?

IS IT SO CRAZY THAT WE'D WANT TO BUILD SOMETHING TO PROTECT OURSELVES FROM SUCH THREATS?

IN CASE THE SUPER HEROES EVER **FAIL?**

SOME PEOPLE IN S.H.I.E.L.D. THINK IT'S CRAZY FOR HUMANITY TO PUT ALL OF ITS FAITH IN A SELF-APPOINTED BAND OF COSTUMED ADVENTURERS.

ALL RESPECT, CAPTAIN, YOU THINK S.H.I.E.L.D. GOT TOO **BIG** AND OVERREACHED?

"HAVE YOU LOOKED AT THE SIZE OF THE AVENGERS ROSTER LATELY?"

THE UPPER WEST SIDE.

OH, MAN...

SOMEBODY DID SOMETHING BAD TO MY HEAD.

=YAWN!=

WHO WAS IT? RED SKULL? THANOS? ZEMO?

OH NO...

ONE GLASS IS ENOUGH FOR ME, JET.

OH, *C'MON,* FALCON--LIVE A LITTLE.

I'VE TRIED THIS WINE BEFORE. ON MY 23RD BIRTHDAY, FATHER GAVE ME SOME.

I REALLY LIKE THE EFFECT THAT IT PRODUCED.

TWENTY-THREE

AVENGERS MANSION HAS STOOD FOR OVER A HUNDRED YEARS.

IN RECENT YEARS IT HAS BEEN HOME TO THE MIGHTIEST BEINGS ON EARTH.

ITS WALLS ARE IMPENETRABLE.

ITS SECURITY INFALLIBLE.

FEW HAVE EVER SUCCESSFULLY BROKEN INTO THIS MANSION--

NONE EVER SO QUICKLY.

A COMPUTER WITHIN THE INTRUDER'S ARMOR HUMS TO LIFE.

A SMALL BLINKING LIGHT INDICATING THE DIRECTION OF HIS TARGET.

BUT HIS TARGET IS NOT ALONE.

EXCUSE ME, SIR...

YOU WANT TO FIGHT THIS OUT?

WHOOOSH

I CAN WORK WITH THAT.

KROKK

OOF--!

BUT YOU'LL HAVE TO DO BETTER.

I'VE WAITED FAR TOO LONG TO BE DETERRED BY CLUMSY BLOWHARDS.

EXCUSE ME, NEW FRIEND, I'VE SCOURED STEVE'S ITINERARY--

GHRAGH!

WOOOOSH

DIRTY IS *PREDICTABLE.*

I WAS TRAINED TO FIGHT *SMART.*

NOT *TOO* SMART.

GOT CLOSE.

HOOF!

UNDER-ESTIMATED YOUR TARGET.

TWOKK

NOW, IF YOU KNOW WHAT'S GOOD FOR YOU-- STAY DOWN.

I'M AFRAID I CAN'T...

...I WAS TAUGHT TO *ALWAYS* STAND UP.

W-WHAT DID YOU JUST SAY?

I ALWAYS STAND UP.

LIKE MY DAD TAUGHT ME.

IT... IT'S...?

I-I WATCHED YOU DIE...

I FELL INTO ZOLA'S BIO-MASS TANK.

SAME STUFF I'M MADE FROM. CODED TO REGENERATE--

OH, THANK GOD... THANK SWEET GOD.

NEXT UP ON WORLD'S **STRANGEST** HOME INVASIONS...

IT'S STRANGER THAN IT SEEMS, TONY.

I TRIED TO EXPLAIN...

GENTLEMEN, I'D LIKE TO INTRODUCE YOU ALL TO MY SON.

MEET IAN ROGERS.

SON?!

BOY, I AM OUT OF THE LOOP.

IAN, I-I CAN'T TELL YOU WHAT A RELIEF--

WE HAVE TO DEAL WITH IT ALL LATER, DAD. TIME IS SHORT.

YOU'VE SEEN ZOLA'S TOWER?

JUST.

THE LAST TEN YEARS I'VE DONE EVERYTHING I COULD TO DISMANTLE THAT PSYCHOPATH'S BREEDING CHAMBERS.

HE'S EVOLVED THEM, MILLIONS OF TIMES OVER.

THE ARMY HE'S GROWN IS UNLIKE ANYTHING I'VE SEEN BEFORE.

WHEN I DISCOVERED HE WAS PLANNING ON INVADING EARTH, I INFILTRATED HIS TOWER, TRIED TO SHUT IT DOWN, BUT I WAS TOO LATE TO--

STEVE, IT'S FALCON-- ARE YOU THERE?!

I'M HERE, SAM.

WE'VE GOT SOME BAD TROUBLE.

WE JUST PICKED IT UP. TONY SENT OUT A GENERAL PRIORITY ALERT TO ALL AVENGERS.

WE WERE GETTING READY TO HEAD OUT WHEN WE HAD A BIT OF AN... INTERRUPTION.

TWENTY-FOUR

OOF--!

TWUNG

YOUR OLD MAN IS A *BUMMER*.

SAM, THIS INVASION-- IT'S ALL JUST A *DIVERSION!*

YOU HAVE TO WARN THEM!

STEVE, YOU THERE? ENGAGING WITH ZOLA--WE'RE OUT OF THE TOWER.

I'VE GOT VISUAL, SAM.

THE AVENGERS AND EVERYONE ELSE ARE BUSY WITH THE MUTATES.

WITH ZOLA YOU NEED TO GO IN HEAVY, GET THROUGH THAT ARMOR AND *TEAR* AT CIRCUITS--

LISTEN--JET THINKS THERE IS SOMETHING ELSE HAPPENING, SOMETHING *BIG.*

AND THAT'S NOT ALL...

...SHARON IS UP THERE, STEVE. SHE'S IN THE TOWER-- *ALIVE.*

I USUALLY ENJOY AN AFTERNOON IN CENTRAL PARK.

DON'T FIND MUCH TIME FOR LEISURE THESE DAYS--

WHAT WITH BEING REALLY IMPORTANT AND EVERYTHING.

I GUESS YOU HAVE TO TAKE IT WHERE YOU CAN GET IT.

GAZAK

THE AVENGERS ARE GOING TO HAVE TO TAKE CARE OF THE MUTATES, SON, I JUST GOT WORD FROM SAM--

SHARON CARTER IS ALIVE IN THE TOWER, SURROUNDED BY MUTATES.

MOM?

MOM?

IAN, WHAT THE *HEL* GOING ON?

IAN, WE'VE GOT A SITUATION.

THAT RIGHT, DAD...?

I HADN'T NOTICED.

SKROK

E RAISED ME AFTER YOU LEFT.

BUT AFTER THE LAST RAID ON ZOLA'S NEW TOWER--

I THOUGHT SHE WAS DEAD.

LONG STORY-- NOT REALLY ONE I CAN TELL RIGHT NOW.

BUT REST EASY--

I'LL GET MOM OUT OF THERE.

YOU WOULD DOOM MY DAUGHTER WITH YOUR IDEALS!

SHACKLE HER TO THE PLEBEIAN AND CORRUPT!

GROOOOM

DOOOOOOM

SHE'S NO ONE'S PUPPET, ZOLA--

SKROKK

--ESPECIALLY NOT HER FATHER'S.

SAVE YOUR PREACHING!

THIS IS NOT A MATTER TO BE SETTLED WITH WORDS--

COULDN'T AGREE MORE.

KRASHH

STAY STILL, LITTLE ONE.

WANTS THEM SWEET BLOODS.

GET THAT MURDER!

YAH--!

HROOF--!

FAST YES! STILLS YOU D--

SRUKK

MOM--! I THOUGHT WE'D LOST YOU.

DAD, YOU THERE?

WE'VE GOT A PROBLEM.

THE MUTATES ARE JUST BAIT-- ZOLA'S WAY OF LURING ALL OF THE AVENGERS INTO ONE PLACE.

IT'S A BOMB, DAD.

BIG ENOUGH TO WIPE OUT THE CITY AND EVERYONE IN IT.

SAM, I JUST GOT WORD FROM IAN FROM INSIDE THE TOWER.

THIS IS ALL A RUSE-- ZOLA HAS A BOMB.

WE NEED TO EVACUATE THE CITY, GET EVERYONE OUT OF HERE BEFORE HE HAS A CHANCE TO SET IT OFF.

WHY HASN'T HE DETONATED IT YET?

HE MUST BE AFTER SOMETHING--

JET...

ZOLA CONTROLS EVERYTHING REMOTELY THROUGH HIS TELEPATHIC ANTENNAE, EVEN HIS MUTATES.

THAT'S GOING TO BE HOW HE TRIGGERS THE BOMB WHEN HE'S READY.

I'VE GIVEN YOU EVERYTHING! YOU ARE THE ONLY LOVE I HAVE IN MY HEART, JET!

PLEASE-- WE MUST LEAVE HERE!

WE MUST--

WITHOUT YOUR TELEPATHIC BROADCAST DOOHICKEY I GUESS YOU WON'T BE ABLE TO ACTIVATE THAT SECRET BOMB.

NO!

IMBECILE! THE BOMB ACTIVATES *AUTOMATICALLY* IF MY CONNECTION IS SEVERED!

I HAD HOPED TO *SPARE* MY DAUGHTER FROM THE FATE OF THIS *DECAYING PIT,* BUT DUE TO *YOU--*

00.00.30

"--SHE WILL DIE LIKE THE REST."

DAD, THE BOMB'S TRIPWIRE *JUST* WENT OFF-- IT'S SET TO BLOW IN *THIRTY SECONDS!*

TONY! LISTEN TO ME--THERE'S A BOMB SET TO DETONATE INSIDE THE TOWER IN SECONDS--

--GET IT OUT OF THE CITY!

ON IT.

NO--YOU MUST *STAY* FOR THE BROTHER-HOOD!

I AM THE *YOU*--!

I AM THE ONE WHO HAS BEEN WAITING A *MILLION* REBIRTHS--

GHRAGHH--!

--WAITING FOR WE TO DIE AS ONE!

IAN, IRON MAN IS DOWN, I CAN'T GET ANYONE TO YOU--*CAN YOU DEFUSE IT?!*

FIFTEEN SECONDS LEFT... I-I DON'T THINK SO...

THIS IS ZOLA--THERE'S NOT GOING TO BE A WAY TO STOP IT NOW.

NO. PROBABLY NOT.

BUT WE CAN GET IT FAR ENOUGH AWAY.

WHAT ARE YOU DOING, SAM?

ONLY THING TO DO.

WHERE ARE YOU GOING--?!

UP.

SAM, WHAT ARE YOU DOING?

YOU AND SHARON DESERVE SOME PEACE, STEVE.

PROMISE ME YOU'LL FIND SOME?

TAKE SOME TIME-- YOU KNOW-- SMELL THE FLOWERS.

WHO
IS THE
NEW
CAPTAIN
AMERICA?

TWENTY-FIVE

I REMEMBER THE FIRST TIME I MET SAM WILSON AS CLEARLY AS IF IT WAS YESTERDAY.

HE WAS HELPING A BAND OF SUBJUGATED VILLAGERS FIGHT FOR THEIR FREEDOM AGAINST THE RED SKULL.

EVEN AFTER I ARRIVED HE *INSISTED* ON HELPING FIGHT.

HE WAS USED TO FIGHTING.

SAM HAD BEEN THROUGH TERRIBLE ADVERSITY.

LOST BOTH PARENTS TO VIOLENCE AT A YOUNG AGE.

HE RAISED HIS BROTHER AND SISTER.

SUPPORTED THEM.

BUT HE NEVER SUCCUMBED TO BITTERNESS.

HE USED THE TEACHINGS OF HIS PARENTS, A MINISTER AND COMMUNITY ORGANIZER, AS THE STANDARD BY WHICH TO LIVE.

IN A WORLD THAT HAD SHOWN HIM PREJUDICE AND HEARTBREAK...

...SAM WILSON CONTINUOUSLY STOOD UP.

GIVING EVERYTHING HE HAD TO TRY AND SHAPE THE WORLD INTO THE ONE THAT HIS FATHER DREAMED OF.

HE DEDICATED HIMSELF TO THE SERVICE OF THOSE IN NEED.

AS THE FALCON HE'S BEEN RIGHT AT MY SIDE-- FIGHTING ON THE FRONT LINES--FOR ALL THESE YEARS.

NO MAGIC HAMMER.

NO SUPER-SOLDIER SERUM.

JUST A MAN.

A MAN DEDICATED TO SHOWING WHAT ONE PERSON COULD ACCOMPLISH AFTER A LIFETIME OF MISFORTUNE.

SAM WILSON'S ALWAYS BEEN A *HERO*...

...TODAY, HE BECAME SOMETHING MORE.

HE COULDN'T HAVE CARED FOR YOU, JET. NONE OF THEM COULD.

YOU ARE A ZOLA. TO THEM--YOU WILL ALWAYS BE SUSPECT.

WHAT THE HELL DO YOU KNOW ABOUT ANYTHING?

A TINY LITTLE MAN SO SCARED OF THE WORLD YOU CREATED ARMOR TO HIDE FROM IT!

A WALKING EMBODIMENT OF THE ENORMOUS EGO MASKING YOUR TRUE COWARDICE!

YOU BRING ONLY HATE AND MISERY, CLEAVING A SWATH OF SUFFERING IN YOUR WAKE.

THERE IS NOTHING IN YOU BUT UGLINESS.

IF THAT WERE TRUE I'D HAVE SIMPLY DETONATED THE OMEGA BOMB-- I'D HAVE WON!

IT IS BECAUSE OF MY LOVE FOR YOU THAT I FAILED.

"...BUT I HOPE YOU WILL REALIZE YOUR FOLLY BEFORE IT IS TOO LATE."

DEAR GOD...

HE DIDN'T GIVE IT A SECOND THOUGHT.

HE GRABBED THE BOMB AND...

IT WAS JUST IN HIM.

EVERYTHING HE EVER DID WAS FOR SOMEBODY ELSE.

YEAH, I MEAN... THAT DUDE HAD IT *ALL*.

GOOD LOOKS, CHARM... ...THAT CERTAIN *JE NE SAIS QUOI*... THAT MADE LADIES LOVE HIM--

SAM!

AND THAT WAS THE KIND OF FORETHOUGHT THAT LED TO THE GREAT FALCON'S WINGS ABSORBING MOST OF THE BLAST AND SAVING ALL OF NEW YORK CITY.

MAN, HE EVEN HAD THE BRAINS TO ASK TONY STARK TO WHIP HIM UP A PAIR OF VIBRANIUM WINGS AFTER GETTING HIS CAN COOKED BY GUNGNIR.

NOT TO INTERRUPT--

--BUT IT SOUNDS LIKE TONY STARK'S THE *REAL* HERO HERE.

I MEAN, WHAT WITH THE CREATION OF THE VIBRANIUM WINGS AND EVERYTHING.

WE SHOULD GET YOU TO THE MEDICAL LAB IMMEDIATELY.

I WAS KIND OF HOPING YOU'D SUGGEST THE ASGARDIAN CURE-ALL OF MEAD.

SAM!

YOU'RE ALIVE!

YOU'RE ALIVE!

WE'RE ALL ALIVE-- NO THANKS TO YOU.

EXCUSE ME?

RESTRAIN THIS **MENACE** BEFORE SHE CAN DO ANY MORE DAMAGE.

GAG HER WHILE YOU'RE AT IT.

SHARON, PLEASE, I DON'T THINK YOU UNDERSTAND. JET'S BEEN--

SPYING ON YOU, STEVE.

PLOTTING WITH HER FATHER.

YOU... YOU BETRAYED **THEM** FOR HIM?

THAT'S CRAZY!

IF THAT'S CRAZY THEN WHERE DID HE GET THE AVENGERS' DNA TO MAKE HIS MUTATES?

IS IT ANY KIND OF SURPRISE THAT ZOLA KNEW THE **EXACT** MOMENT WHEN STEVE WAS TOO WEAK TO FIGHT BACK?

IS IT ANY KIND OF SURPRISE THAT SHE LET ZOLA GET AWAY?!

SHARON, YOU DON'T UNDERSTAND...THERE **HAS TO BE** ANOTHER EXPLANATION.

MY FATHER WAS RIGHT ABOUT YOU.

RIGHT ABOUT YOU ALL!

JET-- WAIT!

JET, THIS IS A MISTAKE! STOP--LISTEN TO ME!

HE'S NOT THE ANSWER!

TONY, SHE'S HEADING TOWARDS ZOLA'S TOWER-- GRAB HER!

HE'S PLAYED US ALL. THEY *BOTH* HAVE.

I KNOW IT'S *HARD* TO BELIEVE...

YOU DON'T KNOW THE HALF OF IT.

ONE
WEEK
LATER.

THE MINI-CHIMICHANGAS ARE ALL GONE.

THE PIZZA ROLLS TOO.

I THINK IT WAS THE VISION.

MINI-CHIMICHANGAS DO NOT AGREE WITH ME.

THEY EMERGE MUCH LIKE FIRE.

LIKE... DIARRHEA? DO ANDROIDS GET THAT?

AND GAS.

TERRIBLE GAS. IT'S WHY WE BROKE UP.

DO YOU THINK YOU HOLD A COPYRIGHT ON CAPERING ANTICS?

YOU-- YOU'RE KIDDING? IS THAT A JOKE?

HELLO, EVERYONE.

THANK YOU ALL FOR COMING.

WHAT'S THE BIG NEWS, STEVE?

IT'S NOT THAT I'M TOO IMPORTANT TO WASTE MY TIME WITH BOARD MEETINGS...

...BUT I'M TOO IMPORTANT FOR BOARD MEETINGS.

WHAT IS IT, HAWKEYE? HAS EIGHTBALL GONE ON A CRIME SPREE?

THAT IS YOUR ARCH-ENEMY, RIGHT?

ALL RIGHT, CALM DOWN, GRANDPA.

I'M NOT CHANGING YOUR DEPENDS IF YOU GET OVEREXCITED.

OKAY! HEY--LISTEN UP EVERYONE, AN OLD PERSON IS SPEAKING!

YOU'RE BEING OBTUSE.

JUST JOKING. TENSION-RELIEVING STUFF, YOU HAVE A PROGRAM FOR THAT?

I UNDERSTAND HUMOR, CLINT. DO YOU?

MAYBE IF YA ASK NICELY, SPIDEY COULD WRITE YA SOME NEW MATERIAL, CLINT?

UHH... I SORT OF WORK IMPROV, ROGUE.

SEAT OF MY PANTS, CLEVER ON THE FLY...

OKAY, SPIDEY JUST SELF-APPLIED "CLEVER" AND I'M THROUGH BEING ABUSED--

STEVE, YOU WERE BORING US?

YES, WELL, AS YOU ALL CAN SEE, I'VE AGED...A BIT. AND WITH NO SUPER-SOLDIER SERUM...

I CAN NO LONGER SERVE AS CAPTAIN AMERICA.

I'M TAKING ON A NEW TITLE--

HENCEFORTH I WILL BE KNOWN AS GENERAL GERIATRIC!

NOTHING?

SOMEBODY WANT TO MAKE FUN OF THAT JOKE? TAKE THE HEAT OFF ME?

UGH--THAT WAS REALLY BAD, STEVE.

ANYWAY, BAD JOKE ASIDE, THE HARD TRUTH IS...

I CAN'T WEAR THE COLORS OR FIGHT ON THE FIELD ANY LONGER.

BUT I CAN STILL LEAD AND PLAN TO.

ONCE AN AVENGER-- ALWAYS AN AVENGER.

STILL, PRETTY SEXY COSTUME, RIGHT?

COULD USE SOME SEQUINS, **NOTHING** MORE PATRIOTIC THAN SEQUINS.

NOT SEQUINS.

IT DOES FEEL LIKE IT'S MISSING SOMETHING, SAM.

WOW.

YEAH.

THAT.

THANK YOU, STEVE.

SHE COULDN'T BE IN BETTER HANDS.

I'M NOT FOR SPEECHES...

...NEVER HAVE BEEN ANYWAY.

AYE! THEN **ENOUGH** SPEAKING!

JUST GIVE THEM WHAT THEY WANT, SAM.

MARVEL 75TH ANNIVERSARY SPECIAL CELEBRATION #1

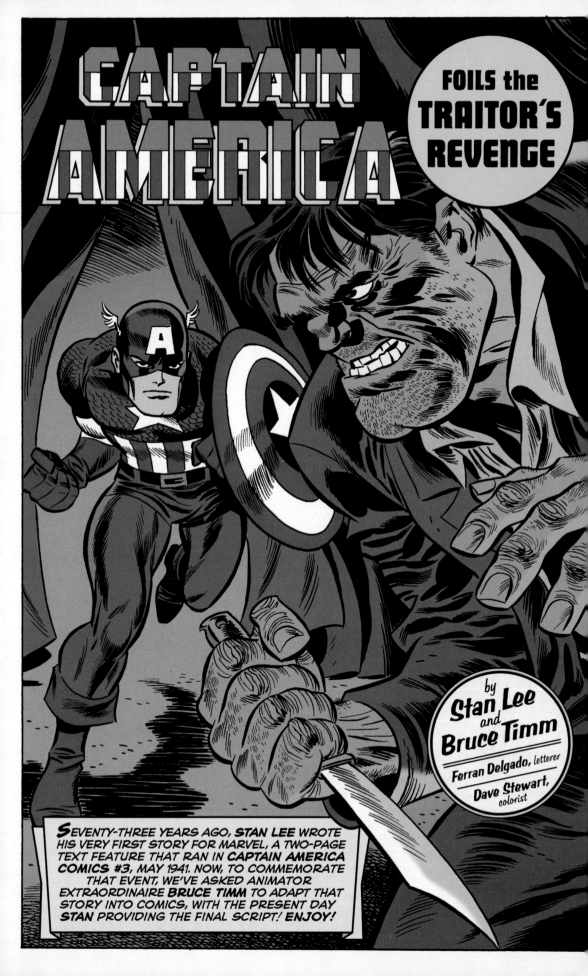

CAPTAIN AMERICA

FOILS the TRAITOR'S REVENGE

by **Stan Lee** and **Bruce Timm**

Ferran Delgado, *letterer*

Dave Stewart, *colorist*

SEVENTY-THREE YEARS AGO, STAN LEE WROTE HIS VERY FIRST STORY FOR MARVEL, A TWO-PAGE TEXT FEATURE THAT RAN IN CAPTAIN AMERICA COMICS #3, MAY 1941. NOW, TO COMMEMORATE THAT EVENT, WE'VE ASKED ANIMATOR EXTRAORDINAIRE BRUCE TIMM TO ADAPT THAT STORY INTO COMICS, WITH THE PRESENT DAY STAN PROVIDING THE FINAL SCRIPT! ENJOY!

AT U.S. ARMY CAMP LEHIGH -- A DRAMATIC SCENE.

THERE IS **NO** PLACE IN THIS ARMY CAMP FOR THE LIKES OF YOU, **HAINES!** YOU HAVE **LIED, CHEATED, SPIED** AND **STOLEN!**

YOUR CONDUCT IS NO LONGER **TOLERABLE** -- I'M GIVING YOU A **DISHONORABLE DISCHARGE!**

GOSH, STEVE! I'VE NEVER SEEN COLONEL STEVENS SO **ANGRY!**

HAINES LOOKS PLENTY **MAD** TOO, **BUCKY!**

OKAY, COLONEL, I'LL GET OUT, BUT YOU AIN'T SEEN THE LAST OF **ME!**

MARK MY WORDS -- **YOU'LL PAY FOR THIS!**

I'LL GET MY **REVENGE** ON THAT LOUSY, NO-GOOD CREEP!

I WOULDN'T ACT LIKE THAT IF I WERE YOU, HAINES!

THAT MAN YOU'RE INSULTING WEARS THE UNIFORM OF THE **UNITED STATES ARMY!**

MOUTH OFF LIKE THAT AGAIN...

...AND I GUARANTEE YOU'LL **REGRET** IT!

HERE ARE THE CAMP GATES!

NOW **BEAT** IT!

YEAH, YEAH, I'M GOIN'...

...BUT I'LL BE **BACK!**

2.

LATER THAT NIGHT...

GOSH, STEVE, DON'T YOU *EVER* LOSE A GAME? I'VE FORGOTTEN WHAT IT FEELS LIKE TO WIN!

TELL YOU WHAT, KID...

...SUPPOSE YOU BORROW A BOOK ON *"HOW TO PLAY CHECKERS"* AND READ IT. THAT'LL GIVE ME A CHANCE FOR SOME *SHUT-EYE!*

YOU DON'T KNOW HOW *TIRED* IT MAKES ME TO BEAT YOU ALL THE TIME!

HEY!

OKAY, SQUIRT, IF IT'S A PILLOW FIGHT YOU WANT--

HOW D'YA KNOW I AIN'T GOT A *BRICK* IN THIS ONE?

WAIT!

DID YOU *HEAR* THAT?

WHAT IS IT, STEVE?

IT'S *HAINES* -- AND TWO *OTHER* GOONS! HEADING TOWARDS THE *COLONEL'S TENT!*

LET'S GO!

YOU GUYS STAY HERE AND KEEP A LOOK-OUT...

...I'LL TAKE CARE OF MR. HIGH-AND-MIGHTY!

NOT WHILE *CAPTAIN AMERICA* IS ON THE JOB!

HERE'S A G.I. WELCOME FOR YOU PUNKS!

CAPTAIN AMERIC-- *UGH!*

STRIKE ONE -- TWO -- THREE --

I'LL 'ASH 'ER 'EAD 'N!

SOK!

-- YOU'RE OUT!

HEY, CAP!

HAINES IS GETTING AWAY!

I'LL GET HIM!

4.

6.

'S LUCKY THE COLONEL'S NOT A LIGHT SLEEPER!

ALTHOUGH HE MIGHT HAVE ENJOYED THE ACTION!

SORRY I WAS TOO BUSY TO *HELP* YOU, BUCKY.

IT'S OKAY, CAP.

I JUST HOPE I WASN'T TOO *ROUGH* WITH 'EM!

THE NEXT MORNING...

ROGERS, THIS MORNING I FOUND THREE MEN TIED UP OUTSIDE MY TENT, WITH A NOTE SAYING "REGARDS FROM CAPTAIN AMERICA AND BUCKY"!

YOU HAVE THE TENT *NEXT* TO MINE-- DID YOU *HEAR* ANYTHING?

NO, SIR. I WAS SOUND *ASLEEP.*

ASLEEP!!

CAPTAIN AMERICA AND BUCKY MOPPED UP THREE MEN BY *THEMSELVES* AND SAVED MY *LIFE...*

...AND *YOU WERE ASLEEP!*

OH, WHY CAN'T I HAVE SOLDIERS LIKE CAPTAIN AMERICA INSTEAD OF *YOU?*

'NUFF SAID!

CAPTAIN AMERICA FOILS the TRAITOR'S REVENGE

By Stan Lee

"I'm sorry, Haines, but there is no place in this army camp for the likes of you. You have lied, cheated, spied, and stolen. Your conduct is no longer tolorable and I'm giving you a dishonorable discharge. Now get out!"

Private Steve Rogers, doing sentry duty nearby, was watching the scene interestedly. He had never seen Colonel Stevens so angry; and Lou Haines, too, was threateningly mad. The muscular giant shook his enormous fist at the Colonel.

"O.K. Colonel," snarled Lou, "I'll get out. But let me warn you now, you ain't seen the last of me! I'll get even somehow. Mark my words, you'll pay for this!" Haines walked toward the camp gates, muttering insults under his breath.

Suddenly Haines felt a strong hand grasp his arm. He looked around into the flashing eyes of Steve Rogers! "I wouldn't act like that if I were you," murmured Steve, softly, "you were insulting a man in the uniform of the United States Army! Here are the camp gates; now beat it!"

Haines left, but there was a look of hate in his eyes which Steve could not help but notice!

* * * * *

Later that evening, Steve Rogers was sitting in his tent playing checkers with his young side-kick, Bucky, the camp mascot. Bucky looked disappointed.

"Gosh, Steve," wailed Bucky,

"don't you EVER lose a game I've forgotten what it feels lik to win."

Steve smiled cheerfully. "I' tell you what, kid: suppose yo borrow a book on 'how to pla checkers' and read it. That' give me a chance to get som shut-eye. You don't know hov tired it makes me to beat yo all the time!"

Steve ducked just in time to dodge the pillow that Bucky threw at him. "Why, you littl squirt," he grinned, "I ought to put you over my knee!"

"Oh yeah, you big palooka? You and what other army?" Bucky picked up another pillow and was holding it ready

Suddenly Steve's smile left his face and he put his fingers

to his lips "Listen," he whispered.

Bucky put down the pillow and was silent. He knew that Steve's sensitive hearing must have detected something important! Then Steve spoke:

"There it is again, Bucky. Three pairs of footsteps outside Colonel Stevens' tent. We'd better look into this!"

In an instant, both Steve and Bucky peeled off their outer uniforms, and seconds later they stood revealed as CAPTAIN AMERICA and BUCKY, Sentinals Of Our Shores! "Let's go!" cried CAPTAIN AMERICA!

The two trouble hunters stole from their tent and noiselessly trod to Colonel Stevens' quarters. Outside his tent were three tough-looking thugs!

"Will we all rush him at once?" asked the first. Captain America saw that the man he was talking to was Lou Haines! "Naw," sneered Haines, "you guys stay here and keep 'chickee'. I'll go in and tend to him myself!" Then Captain America noticed that Haines was holding a wicked-looking knife in his hand!

"Not a second to lose!" cried the Red White and Blue Knight as he raced toward the three assassins like an avenging hurricane.

Lou Haines was the first to see the twin-tornadoes rushing at him. "Take care of these two fancy-pants," he ordered his men, "I'll attend to the Colonel in a second!"

Haines' two accomplices grinned as they watched Captain

America ; and Bucky speeding toward them. They took out their revolvers and prepared to fire But Captain America suddenly picked up Bucky by his arms and swung him right into the two thugs, knocking their guns out of reach. "All right, Bucky, m'lad," he cried, "see how brave they are without their toys!" Then he dashed into the tent.

Inside the tent, the American Avenger saw Lou Haines about to plunge his knife into the sleeping Colonel's heart! There wasn't time for Captain America to reach Haines before the evil deed could be done. But with the speed of thought, he sent his shield spinning through the air to the other end of the tent where it smacked the knife out of Haines' hand!

Then the mighty crime-fighter leaped at Haines and landed a blow at his head. But the traitorous ex-soldier seemed to just shake off the blow and he grabbed Captain America by the throat with his tremendous fingers. As Haines forced more and more pressure into his grip, Captain America began to get weaker and weaker. His eyes grew dim and it became difficult for him to breathe. But he managed to summon all his remaining strength into one last effort, and brought his right fist up under Haines' jaw with enough force to fell an ox. No human being could have stood that blow, and Haines instantly relaxed his grip and sank to the floor — unconscious!

Outside the tent, Captain America found the other two crooks tied back-to-back, and

Bucky was standing over them, patting their heads! "I do hope I wasn't too rough with them, Cap," said the gallant lad.

* * * * *

The next morning Colonel Stevens was talking with Private Rogers. "Rogers," he said, "this morning I found three men tied outside my tent with a note pinned on them, reading: 'Regards from Captain America and Bucky'. Now you have the tent next to mine; did you hear anything last night?"

"No, Sir," answered Steve, "I was sound asleep."

"Asleep!" roared the Colonel, "Captain America and Bucky mopped up three armed men by themselves and saved my life – and YOU were asleep! Oh, why can't I have some soldiers like Captain America in this army – instead of YOU!"

But Colonel Stevens didn't notice the grin on Private Rogers' face as he left the tent!

#22 75TH ANNIVERSARY SKETCH VARIANT BY ALEX ROSS

#22 75TH ANNIVERSARY VARIANT BY ALEX ROSS

#25 VARIANT BY STEVE McNIVEN & MORRY HOLLOWELL

#25 VARIANT BY ADAM HUGHES

#25 VARIANT BY JOHN TYLER CHRISTOPHER

CAPTAIN AMERICA/FALCON DESIGNS BY CARLOS PACHECO

p red outside
wing

black inside
of wing

CAPTAIN AMERICA 22 COVER A PACHECO

#22 COVER PENCILS BY CARLOS PACHECO

CAPTAIN AMERICA 23 COVER PACHECO

ROOM FOR LOGO

#23 COVER SKETCH & PENCILS BY CARLOS PACHECO

#25 COVER PENCILS & INKS BY STUART IMMONEN

#22 PAGES 2-3 PENCILS BY CARLOS PACHECO

CAPTAIN AMERICA 23   21   PACHECO

#23 PAGE 20 INKS BY MARIANO TAIBO

#24 PAGE 13 ART BY CARLOS PACHECO & MARIANO TAIBO

#25 PAGE 20 ART BY CARLOS PACHECO & MARIANO TAIBO

#25 PAGE 22 ART BY CARLOS PACHECO & MARIANO TAIBO